Managing Money

Craig E. Blohm

San Diego, CA

LONGWOOD PUBLIC LIBRARY

About the Author

Craig E. Blohm has written numerous books and magazine articles for young readers. He and his wife, Desiree, reside in Tinley Park, Illinois.

© 2020 ReferencePoint Press, Inc.
Printed in the United States

For more information, contact:
ReferencePoint Press, Inc.
PO Box 27779
San Diego, CA 92198
www.ReferencePointPress.com

ALL RIGHTS RESERVED.
No part of this work covered by the copyright hereon may be reproduced or used in any form or by any means—graphic, electronic, or mechanical, including photocopying, recording, taping, web distribution, or information storage retrieval systems—without the written permission of the publisher.

Picture Credits:
Cover: Valua Vitaly/Shutterstock.com
 5: Lisa F. Young/Shutterstock.com
11: Monkey Business Images/Shutterstock.com
12: Iakov Filimonov/Shutterstock.com
19: Casper1774 Studio/Shutterstock.com
23: Bloomicon/Shutterstock.com
26: weedezign/Shutterstock.com
31: Julie Clopper/Shutterstock.com
35: Theethawat Bootmata/Shutterstock.com
38: 9nong/Shutterstock.com
43: Feng Yu/Shutterstock.com
46: BlueSkyImage/Shutterstock.com
51: iStockphoto.com
55: NicoElNino/Shutterstock.com

LIBRARY OF CONGRESS CATALOGING-IN-PUBLICATION DATA

Name: Blohm, Craig E., 1948– author.
Title: Managing Money/by Craig E. Blohm.
Description: San Diego, CA: ReferencePoint Press, [2019] | Series: Teen Life Skills | Audience: Grade 9 to 12. | Includes bibliographical references and index.
Identifiers: LCCN 2019000768 (print) | LCCN 2019004394 (ebook) | ISBN 9781682827505 (eBook) | ISBN 9781682827499 (hardback)
Subjects: LCSH: Finance, Personal—Juvenile literature.
Classification: LCC HG173.8 (ebook) | LCC HG173.8 .B646 2019 (print) | DDC 332.024—dc23
LC record available at https://lccn.loc.gov/2019000768

CONTENTS

Introduction — 4
The Road to Financial Success

Chapter One — 7
Making Money: Build Your Income

Chapter Two — 16
Budgeting: Plan Your Financial Life

Chapter Three — 24
Spending Money: Shop Sensibly

Chapter Four — 33
Credit: Use It Wisely

Chapter Five — 41
Debt: Learn the Pitfalls

Chapter Six — 49
Investing: Increase Your Wealth

Source Notes — 58
For More Information — 61
Index — 63

INTRODUCTION

The Road to Financial Success

By any standard, $258 billion is a lot of money. It can buy twenty nuclear-powered aircraft carriers for the US Navy or a new Toyota Camry for every person living in Pennsylvania. This huge sum of money is also equal to the total amount spent annually by teenagers in the United States, according to a survey by Statistic Brain. For most of America's 42 million teenagers, money is an important part of life. Whether teenagers acquire their money by working at part-time jobs, doing household chores, creating their own home-based or online businesses, or receiving a weekly allowance, their spending habits make them a vital segment of the American economy.

But money is more than simply a means to purchase goods and services. Neale S. Godfrey is the author of numerous books on money, life skills, and values. She stresses that for teenagers, the importance of money is not limited to its buying power but is "a positive force in a system of values. . . . Young people need to learn the value of money, and they need to learn how to incorporate money into an overall philosophy of social, personal, and ethical values."[1]

Acquiring Financial Skills

To learn the value of money, teenagers must acquire a number of financial skills: how to earn money, how to spend it wisely, how to use it to build a solid financial future, and how to recognize and avoid financial pitfalls. Unfortunately, most teens admit that they know little about money management. And it is often unclear where they can acquire good financial advice. "Parents think the schools are doing the training and the schools think the parents are doing the training," says marketing expert Judy Hoberman. "Teens are brought into an environment where you use plastic for most of your big purchases, and if you need cash, you go to a little machine and money comes out."[2]

> "Young people need to learn the value of money, and they need to learn how to incorporate money into an overall philosophy of social, personal, and ethical values."[1]
>
> —Author Neale S. Godfrey

With proper motivation, however, teens can learn the necessary financial skills. A bit of research into how to handle money and create a sound financial plan can give teens a head start in good

Teenagers in the United States spend approximately $258 billion annually. Their spending habits make them a vital part of the economy.

money management habits. These habits, when applied carefully and consistently, can result in a lifetime of financial success.

Of course, financial success can mean different things to different teens. Jack may have entrepreneurial ambitions with the goal of forming his own software company, while Cherise's passion for helping people may lead her to pursue a degree in medicine or family counseling. Other teens might need a job to help out with family expenses or to cover the cost of learning a marketable skill at a community college. While every teenager's situation and financial goals are different, one thing all teens have in common is that they will benefit from learning how to handle money wisely.

The Road Ahead

Graduating from high school opens up a whole new world for teenagers. It is the first step on the road to adulthood, with all the freedom and choices that come with it. But adulthood also comes with responsibilities, and many of these are tied to the management of financial assets. These responsibilities may include paying for college, finding a job, paying taxes, or getting married and having children. Each of these obligations, and many more in an adult's life, require money.

Fortunately, today's teens have more options than their parents had when it comes to managing money. The greatest advance is, of course, the internet. Instead of going to a physical bank or dealing with paying bills by mail, teens can manage bank accounts, purchase goods, invest, and even run an online business from home or anywhere a cell phone can connect to the web. In addition, financial software can make keeping track of a budget, preparing tax forms, and analyzing investments more convenient and less susceptible to error.

There is no better time than the teen years to learn how to manage money. With a solid base of financial knowledge, teenagers can look forward to a smooth ride on the lifelong road to financial success.

CHAPTER ONE

Making Money: Build Your Income

Over the years there have been many sayings about money that are so often repeated that they have become clichés:

"Money doesn't grow on trees."

"You get what you pay for."

"A penny saved is a penny earned."

"You can't take it with you."

As trite as these sayings may be, they have one thing in common: They are all essentially true. While money may lend itself to corny sayings, the fact is that it is one of the most important things in modern life. Without money, manufacturers could not build factories to produce goods (although no one would have money to buy them anyway). Artists could not be paid to create paintings, music, books, or films. Farm crops would rot in the fields for lack of money to buy them.

The importance of money leads to the question of how to acquire this essential commodity. Since money truly does not grow on trees, teens must find a way to get the money they need to live in the world's money-based economy.

Finding a Job

A teenager's number one job is school, because getting a good education is the most important factor in preparing for a productive and meaningful life. But being a teenager also means needing or wanting the things that money can buy. In many cases it can also mean helping out with family expenses. The traditional way for teens to acquire money is to earn it with a part-time or summer job. These jobs may include working at a fast-food restaurant, stocking items at a grocery store, delivering pizzas, or working in a retail store as a sales associate or cashier.

Years ago Jeff Bliss, who is now a radio show cohost, began working when he was thirteen years old. He sold peanuts and soda at a local raceway, using his own money to buy the products and then selling them at a higher price to make his profit. Bliss put in fourteen-hour days, which was hard work for a thirteen-year-old. Today, under federal labor laws, fourteen is the youngest age for employment, although some states have set higher minimum ages. But at any age, jobs such as babysitting, lawn mowing, and working for one's parents can bring in needed money.

Looking for a part-time job requires work and determination. It may be more difficult if you've never worked before, but there are ways to make a job search successful. According to employment expert Alison Doyle, getting noticed is a good way to begin a job search. "Tell everyone you know you are looking for a job. Many jobs aren't advertised, and you may be able to get a good job lead from a friend or family member. The more people you tell, the better your chances of finding a job. Also, try stopping in at local businesses, and ask if they are hiring."[3]

> "Tell everyone you know you are looking for a job. Many jobs aren't advertised, and you may be able to get a good job lead from a friend or family member. The more people you tell, the better your chances of finding a job. Also, try stopping in at local businesses, and ask if they are hiring."[3]
>
> —Employment expert Alison Doyle

It helps to be flexible by not limiting your job search to a particular type of job or industry: Being open to various kinds of work will help in a crowded employment market. Flexibility also applies to working hours; more availability can mean the difference between getting hired and being passed over. Other important tasks you should think about when looking for a job include creating a résumé, doing research to become familiar with a prospective employer, and dressing appropriately for job interviews. Doyle calls this last item the Grandma Rule. "If your grandmother would like your interview outfit," she says, "you are dressed properly."[4]

There are also many online resources for teenagers seeking part-time or summer employment. Sites such as Snag, GrooveJob, and Craigslist are good sources for job leads.

The Vanishing Summer Job

Every spring the end of the school year heralds a summer of fun and leisure for teenagers. It also used to mean a chance to make some extra money at a summer job. But today working is no longer the definitive summer activity it once was.

In 1968 some 60 percent of teenagers either had summer jobs or were actively seeking work. By 2016 that number had plunged to 35 percent. Why the drastic drop in teen summer employment? Some people assumed that teenagers were simply getting lazier and would rather spend their summers at the beach or hanging out with friends. But it turns out that teens are anything but lazy; in fact, they are working hard during the summer—at academic pursuits.

More high school students today are planning to go to college. Facing tough college entrance requirements, many of them are taking advanced placement courses in the summer to add to their résumé. In 2017 the Bureau of Labor Statistics reported that the percentage of sixteen- to nineteen-year-olds taking summer classes tripled in the previous twenty years. So, while you may see fewer teens working at fast-food restaurants this summer, you'll probably find them working hard in the classroom instead.

Pros and Cons of a Part-Time Job

While earning money is an important part of working at a part-time job, there are other advantages. Part-time jobs can teach teens valuable lessons that will help them throughout their working lives. The skills gained through work can include managing time and money, working with others as a team, dealing with customers and employers, and setting priorities. Part-time jobs also help establish a record of good work habits, which is important when seeking full-time employment later. Looking back on his raceway job, Bliss says, "I think I learned more . . . about economics and personal finance at that job than I did in any classes I had."[5]

Of course, if you're working, you need to find a proper balance between school and work. Both are serious commitments that require dedication, energy, and above all, time. "It's all about balance," notes Scott Dobroski of the online job search site Glassdoor. "If [a teen's] grades are slipping, then that does take priority over work."[6] Evaluate your current commitments to school (including homework and extracurricular activities), as well as family and leisure-time interests, to determine if a part-time job will fit into your schedule. It may be wise to limit the number of working hours to fifteen per week or fewer to make sure your job and other commitments can work together.

Another consideration is the possibility of making too much money. This may seem illogical, but earning too much can actually hurt a high school student's eligibility for financial assistance for college. Need-based loans for higher education are determined by household income, including money earned by the student. The more a family makes, the less loan money will be available. For the 2018–2019 school year, for example, a student could earn $6,570 without affecting financial aid. Making more than that would lower the amount of aid available.

Working a part-time or summer job can help you discover what career areas you might want to pursue as an adult. Finding a job that fits with your interests and personality may be difficult

A teenager's number one job is school. Getting a good education is the most important factor in preparing for a productive and meaningful life.

at first, but doing what you love can pay dividends in the long run. For example, if you are outgoing and enjoy meeting new people, you might try a sales or customer service position. Teens with an artistic flair may find a rewarding part-time job in a marketing or advertising firm. Animal lovers might discover working at a pet shop or veterinary clinic to be their ideal job.

Income and Deductions

Once hired, you will be confronted with learning the details of pay, deductions, and income taxes. Part-time jobs usually pay a minimum hourly wage set by the federal government, which was $7.25 in 2018. Many states, however, set their own minimum wages that exceed the federal guideline. Companies may also give their employees more than the minimum wage. For example, Amazon began paying its workers $15 per hour in November 2018. Wages for jobs that involve tipping by customers, such as restaurant wait staff, are exceptions to this minimum. Pay for these jobs can be as low as $2.13 an hour, since it is expected that tips will bring the total to the minimum wage. In many cases generous tips can push this pay above the minimum wage.

After working for a week or two, you will experience an important rite of passage to adulthood: receiving your first paycheck. This may be an actual paper check or a direct deposit into a sav-

Wages for jobs that involve tipping, such as restaurant wait staff, are exempt from minimum wage laws. However, tips will usually push the total pay for these jobs above minimum wage.

ings or checking account. But whatever its form, a paycheck can be confusing, with unfamiliar terms such as FICA, gross, and net. Probably the first thing that stands out is that the amount on the check is less than the total amount, or gross pay, earned. Certain deductions are automatically taken out of each paycheck. Federal income tax is deducted, as are state and local taxes in some areas. FICA, which stands for Federal Insurance Contributions Act, deducts an amount for Medicare and Social Security, programs that most people rely on in their later years. Other amounts may be deducted for uniforms or other expenses required for work. After all the deductions are taken from the gross pay, the amount left is the net, also called take-home pay. This is yours to save, spend, or invest any way you choose.

Getting that first paycheck is a thrilling experience. But there are other ways to create income. If you are a self-starter and have a good imagination, starting a business may be the way to go.

Be Your Own Boss

Author and financial expert Robert T. Kiyosaki says he began to create his own businesses early. As a youth, he and a friend started a business by creating a comic-book lending library. "I cleaned out the spare room in the basement," Kiyosaki says, "and in it we opened our comic-book library and reading room. We charged ten cents admission to any kid who wanted to come in and read comics during two hours each weekday that our library was open."[7]

Starting a business can be risky but also rewarding. Turning an idea into a profitable business and working as your own boss is a lifelong goal for many people. Properly motivated teenagers can begin that process and earn money while still in high school. To see if running a business is a practical option for you, one of the easiest ways to start is to charge for services such as housecleaning, dog walking, mowing lawns, and shoveling snow. Create advertising flyers to distribute to neighbors' houses or use word of mouth to promote the business.

Ice Cream Entrepreneur

Fifteen-year-old Mik Bushinski played hockey for Shattuck-St. Mary's School in Faribault, Minnesota. In the summer of 2009, he needed to find a job that would allow him to set work hours around his hockey practices. Finding no suitable employment, Bushinski started his own ice cream sales business. "We had lived in Woodbury for 20 years," he recalls, "and hadn't seen ice cream trucks very often. . . . The community was growing and had a lot of families with children, so it looked like a good fit." With a loan from his uncle, Bushinski started with one truck, naming his new business Mik Mart Ice Cream.

As his business boomed, Mik added a second truck and enlisted his family to help out. By 2017 Mik Mart was an established business with five trucks, two pushcarts, and twelve high school and college student employees. The company even has ice cream vending machines. Mik's advice for teenagers who want to start a business: Find a product you believe in, be prepared to put in the time necessary for success, and have a solid financial plan.

Quoted in Kara McGuire, *The Teen Money Manual: A Guide to Cash, Credit, Spending, Saving, Work, Wealth, and More*. North Mankato, MN: Capstone, 2015, p. 35.

Teens who have specific talents or skills can use them to make money while doing something they enjoy and are good at. Items created with crafts such as knitting, painting, or woodworking can be sold at local craft fairs, art shows, and consignment shops. Offering crafts on websites like Etsy is great for reaching a wider audience, as is creating your own website. For teens with practical mechanical or technical skills, repairing cars, maintaining computers, or designing graphics for print or the web can also be lucrative sources of income. A photography enthusiast with a drone can make a profit shooting aerial photos and videos.

Fifteen-year-old Isaiah Rusk began an online clothing business, inspired by friends in his Houston, Texas, neighborhood who admired his sense of style and sought his advice. "I can go to the thrift store and pick up things that are cool," he explains, "and post them on a website, and if they like it they could buy it." A smart entrepreneur, Rusk expanded his market with advertising. "I got the word out through Twitter and Instagram and Tumblr. Most of my customers aren't even from my area,"[8] he says. Rusk manages his work and school schedules by purchasing inventory on weekends and shipping orders after his homework is done.

Making money is a big step in your path to responsible adulthood. Whether it is earned through a job or a business, received as gifts on special occasions, or obtained as an allowance for doing household chores, you gain a real sense of independence that comes from making decisions on how to use your own money. Such experience gained during the teen years can go a long way to help create a healthy financial future.

> "I can go to the thrift store and pick up things that are cool, and post them on a website, and if they like it they could buy it. I got the word out through Twitter and Instagram and Tumblr. Most of my customers aren't even from my area."[8]
>
> —Teenage entrepreneur Isaiah Rusk

CHAPTER TWO

Budgeting: Plan Your Financial Life

Creating plans is an essential element in numerous areas of life. Architects and engineers draw plans so that buildings and bridges will not collapse. Airline pilots file flight plans to arrive at their destination safely and economically. The latest fashions are planned out well before the first stitch is sewn. One of the most important plans for teenagers to develop is a plan for managing their money: a budget.

What Is a Budget?

While that first paycheck signifies a step toward adulthood, it also comes with the adult question of what to do with the money. Ninth grader Corbin Atack observed the spending habits of some of his classmates. "A lot of them like to go out and buy lunch, because it's a new thing you get to do in high school,"[9] he says. While food is the number one expense category for teenagers, they may also spend their money on a new video game or the latest fashion trend. But those types of impulse purchases will not satisfy for long, and soon the temptation to spend money on other new things will return. Creating a budget will help avoid this cycle of careless spending.

Budgeting does not have to be a dreaded chore or an exercise in advanced math. In fact, 62 percent of students already use some form of budget to track their expenses. Making and following a budget can be a learning experience and a source of satisfaction, not to mention a good way to watch your money work and grow.

A budget is a financial plan that estimates income and expenditures over a period of time, most often on a monthly basis. It allows a person to list money earned and compare it to money spent. A budget usually groups spending into categories such as food, clothing, entertainment, education, and any other category that fits a person's lifestyle. Ideally, expenditures will be equal to or lower than income. At the end of the budget period, any overspending can be evaluated and the budget adjusted to bring expenses more in line with income.

Financial experts agree that budgeting is an essential element of money management, whether for a large corporation, a family, or a teen just starting his or her first paying job. Fortunately, there are a number of ways to create an effective budget.

Budgeting Tools

One of the simplest budgeting methods is the use of envelopes to track cash flow. You label envelopes with various expense categories: food, clothing, entertainment, and so on. Then you put cash into each envelope for the amount to be spent on that category. For example, twenty dollars may go into the food envelope for a week of school lunches, five dollars for movie rentals or downloads, and ten dollars for clothes. As those expenses occur, you take cash from the appropriate envelope to pay for them. When an envelope is empty, no more can be spent on that category of expenses.

The envelope system is a great way to track where your money goes and calls attention to the reality of what things cost in cold, hard cash. Of course, for the system to work, there must be no cheating. The temptation to take a few bucks from one envelope to make an impulse purchase in another category is always there. But according to Steve Scott on his website Develop Good Habits, "The cash envelope system is somewhat akin to having your father standing behind you . . . whispering sensible spending

> "The cash envelope system is somewhat akin to having your father standing behind you ... whispering sensible spending advice over your shoulder ... questioning your need for roasted cashews and bacon flavored potato chips."[10]
>
> —Blogger Steve Scott

advice over your shoulder . . . questioning your need for roasted cashews and bacon flavored potato chips."[10]

Most computers come with a spreadsheet program such as Microsoft Excel already installed. Although it may take some time to learn how to use these programs, they can help categorize expenses and automatically calculate how income is being spent. Other useful budgeting software includes Mvelopes, which digitally mimics the envelope system, and Quicken, a personal finance program that has been around since the earliest personal computers.

Online apps are becoming popular, led by Mint and You Need a Budget (YNAB), which are available for Apple and Android devices. Both apps are great for creating budgets, tracking expenses, and setting financial goals. While Mint is free, YNAB cost $6.99 per month in 2018, although students get the first year free.

Setting Financial Goals

One important advantage of managing money using a budget is the ability to achieve financial goals. Food, clothing, and entertainment are normally recurring expenses easily handled with a budget. But it is also important to set goals for the future and incorporate them into a financial plan. When you're involved in school, work, and social activities, the future may seem far away. But the sooner your future goals are identified and planned for, the greater the chance that the money will be there when those expenses arrive.

Financial goals can be either short term or long term. Short-term goals might include saving up for concert tickets or a new pair of sneakers, while long-term goals could mean putting money away to buy a car or to use for college tuition. "My plan," says high school student Shantrell, "since I got my first job at the age of 16, was to save my money for college and to have at least

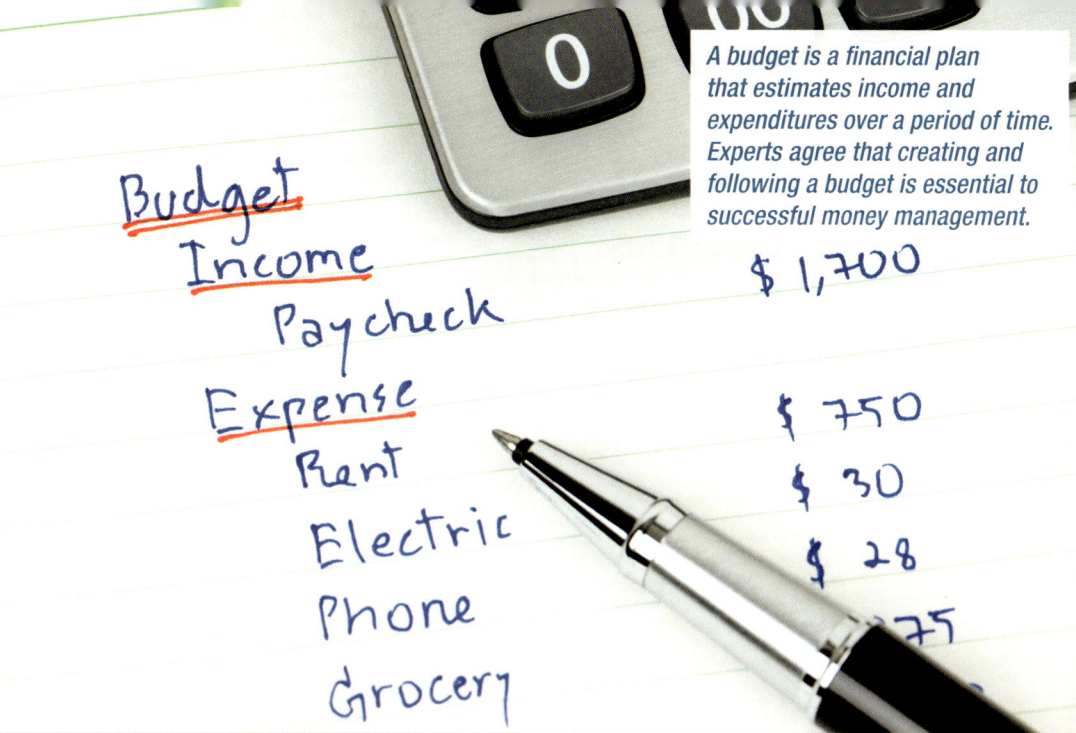

A budget is a financial plan that estimates income and expenditures over a period of time. Experts agree that creating and following a budget is essential to successful money management.

$1,000 in the bank by the end of the year. . . . I continually keep myself on a budget, consisting of buying things I needed—not wanted."[11] By saving some money from each paycheck she received, Shantrell succeeded in achieving her financial goals.

Saving should always be an important part of any budget. Whether using a simple envelope system or a more comprehensive app, a category should be created to help save for the future. Putting a little aside from each paycheck is a good start. Saving money received as gifts, from selling unwanted items, or by doing occasional odd jobs such as mowing lawns or shoveling snow for neighbors can also add to the savings goal. Of course, money saved for future expenses should be kept separate from funds allotted for daily living expenses. One of the best places for keeping money safe is a bank or other savings institution.

Banking Your Money

Traditional bank accounts are a dependable and safe way to save money. Often, parents will open a savings account for a young child even before he or she is aware of the need for one. When you're ready to open a savings or checking account, it's wise to visit several local banks and ask questions about types of student accounts available, the minimum amount needed to maintain the account, and what fees, if any, are charged. Savings accounts typically can be opened by providing an identifying document, such as a driver's license or other photo ID, and an initial deposit of twenty-five or fifty dollars. For teens under eighteen years old, a parent may be required to cosign for the account.

Another good reason for keeping money in a bank is that it earns more money by accumulating interest. Interest is a percent-

You're the Boss!

What would happen if a teenager was put in charge of a family's budget? That's the question an Australian TV program called *Teenage Boss* tries to answer. On the show, teens are given control over their family's budget for one month—and the results are enlightening.

"A coffee machine? What do you want a coffee machine for? What am I going to eat?" These words were spoken by dad Gabriel when his fifteen-year-old son, Michael, came home from the grocery store. The family's $150 food budget had ballooned to $228 with the coffee machine purchase. "Michael is not good with money," Gabriel lamented. *Teenage Boss* was definitely a learning experience for Michael and the other teen bosses, like fourteen-year-old Mitchell, who had no trouble with the math involved but had to learn people skills for dealing with the family.

Eddie Woo, a math teacher and the host of *Teenage Boss*, calls the show "an authentic learning experience." That experience sometimes comes unexpectedly, such as when thirteen-year-old Vasanth had to decide how to pay for his mom's sudden illness. *Teenage Boss* is also a learning experience for the parents, who find themselves dependent on their kids for money.

Quoted in ABC News, "Here's What Happens When Teens Take Control of the Family Budget for a Month," June 22, 2018. www.abc.net.au.

age of the money in the account added on a certain schedule, sometimes monthly or daily. Although the interest rate is usually small—perhaps only 1 or 2 percent—over time it can add up. John, for example, received a bar mitzvah gift of $500 and deposited it in his savings account with the intention of leaving it there to grow. After one year in the bank at an interest rate of 1 percent, John's $500 had grown to $505; after five years he would have over $525. And if John added money to his account from time to time, it would grow even faster.

Certificates of Deposit and Money Market Accounts

While interest on savings and checking accounts make savings grow, teens may wish to consider including certificates of deposit (CDs) and money market accounts in their financial plan to make money grow even faster. With a CD, money is placed in an account for a specified period of time, such as six months, one year, or longer. The money must stay in the CD for that period and may not be withdrawn without paying a substantial penalty. In exchange, the CD earns a higher interest rate than a traditional bank account; the more money deposited and the longer the time period, the higher the rate will be. Like bank accounts, CDs are insured by the federal government, so they are a safe way to earn interest on money that is not immediately needed for budgeted expenses.

Money market accounts are similar to CDs but differ in that they allow a certain number of withdrawals without paying a penalty. Checks are usually provided to make it easy to take funds from the account. Money market accounts require a higher initial deposit, and a minimum balance must be kept in the account to avoid fees.

Banking on the Internet

Traditional brick-and-mortar banks have a physical building, utility bills to pay, and a staff of tellers to assist their customers. In the twenty-first century, the rise of online banking does away with these expenses and passes savings on to the customer. "Online banks cost much less to run than physical banks," says Thomas Porter, who as a college student has reviewed financial products on the web. "Online banks can operate a single central office and manage all of the bank's accounts from one place. That lets them hire fewer employees and take advantage of economies of scale. Online banks then pass those savings on to customers by paying more interest."[12] One of the most popular internet banks is Ally, which was founded in 2001. Like most other internet banks, Ally offers savings and checking accounts, CDs, loans, and other banking products online, as well as 24/7 customer support via phone or chat.

Making a Budget

High school student Christina explains the process she used to set up her first budget.

I have recently learned to set a budget. Four weeks ago, I started my first job, and I have received three paychecks. Out of those paychecks, I have to save 60 percent. Right now, I don't have debt, but soon I will have a car, and with a car comes insurance and gas that I will have to pay for. I also have college to think about. I have to build my savings for college because I want to go to a major university.

My plan is to first save the 60 percent my parents tell me I have to, and then I have to make good choices in the things I spend the rest of my money on. Second, if I can, I will save more of the 40 percent I have left. Right now, my parents make sure that I have food and clothes, so there isn't much else that I need. . . .

In the end, making a budget and saving is not easy, but it is necessary if you want to achieve your goals!

Quoted in Tamsen Butler, *The Complete Guide to Personal Finance for Teenagers and College Students*. Ocala, FL: Atlantic, 2016, p. 115.

Online banks have grown in popularity in the twenty-first century. They operate at a lower cost, which allows them to pay higher interest rates than traditional banks do to attract customers.

Although online banks offer convenience, there are some drawbacks. Some do not offer checking accounts, and it may be difficult or impossible to deposit cash. Also, teens who are new to banking may have questions that would be better answered by talking to a teller in person rather than relying on telephone or online help.

One key to successful financial management is creating a budget that accurately tracks how much money you have and where it goes. And no matter what method is used, your budget should be a reflection of who you are. "Budgets are personal," says financial planner Pamela Capalad. "Your budget should 100% line up to your values and not anyone else's."[13]

> **"Budgets are personal. Your budget should 100% line up to your values and not anyone else's."[13]**
>
> —Financial planner Pamela Capalad

CHAPTER THREE

Spending Money: Shop Sensibly

In the digital age of the twenty-first century, the typical scene of groups of teenagers spending hours roaming through shopping malls is becoming a thing of the past. Many specialty store chains that catered mainly to teens have closed outlets or have even gone bankrupt. Of course, teenagers have not forsaken shopping altogether. According to marketing company JCDecaux, "Teens are important to the U.S. economy since they are most likely to embrace new technology and show the most excitement for current trends that later filter into the mainstream."[14]

Teens have money to spend, but they often make purchases on impulse or by yielding to peer pressure. Both of these are signs that many teens lack the knowledge to wisely handle their own money. Good money management includes making thoughtful decisions about what to spend hard-earned money on and whether purchasing the latest fad item is a smart move to make.

Needs Versus Wants

It is a fact of life that everybody needs things, and everybody wants things as well. Needs are things that are essential to maintain life. These include food, shelter, clothing, health care, and school expenses such as transportation, books, and supplies. Wants are those things you desire after the needs are met: concert tickets, electronic devices, sports equipment, fashion accessories—the list is endless. Although it is important to distinguish between the two, that may not be as easy as it first appears. Erin Huffstetler, who writes about thrifty living for the website Balance, explains:

> "Teens are important to the U.S. economy since they are most likely to embrace new technology and show the most excitement for current trends that later filter into the mainstream."[14]
>
> —Market research company JCDecaux

> The difference between a need and a want is pretty simple—until you set yourself loose in a store. Double chocolate chip ice cream? It's a food, so mark it as a need. That designer T-shirt that fits you perfectly? Well, you need more shirts, so why shouldn't it count as a need, too. It's easy to mix up wants and needs, break your budget, and lose sight of your goal to live frugally.[15]

For most teens, needs are provided for by their parents, while money for wants may come from allowances, gifts, or payment for household chores. Teens who are working may help contribute to family expenses as well as pay for the things they want. But often, many things considered needs may turn out to be wants. Replacing a worn-out pair of sneakers with new ones is certainly a need. Although an expensive pair of Air Jordans or Converse will replace the worn-out shoes, a more reasonably priced pair that does not bear a famous logo will work just as well. Similarly, the need for a caffeine fix can be satisfied with a coffee from Dunkin' just as well as an expensive Starbucks latte.

Knowing the difference between needs and wants is essential to keeping your finances on track. It's hard to give up buying an item that is desirable but unnecessary; being able to do so is a big step toward the adult responsibility of good money management.

Smart Shopping

Becoming a savvy shopper is another important piece of the financial management puzzle. Just because an item is sold at a certain price at one store doesn't mean that it can't be found elsewhere for less. Sales, discounts, coupons, and seasonal merchandising all affect what a consumer will pay for a given item. It takes a bit of work, but finding the lowest price or the best deal should be part of your financial plan.

Comparison shopping is a smart tactic for saving money. Prices can differ from store to store for a variety of reasons. Manufacturers create guidelines for minimum and maximum prices for a product, but it is up to the retailer to set a price within those guidelines. Store location, personnel costs, and local competition all factor into a retailer's pricing decisions. The type of retailer also affects price: A bag of potato chips usually costs more at a convenience store than it does at a full-service grocery store. Ide-

Sales, discounts, and coupons all affect what one will ultimately pay for an item. Making an effort to find the lowest price or the best deal should be part of any financial plan.

Shopping with Apps

There is an astonishing number of apps available today for smartphones and tablets. The two major outlets, the App Store and Google Play, offer more than 4 million apps, ranging from games to utilities. Among these are apps that can help teenagers become smart shoppers, save money, and maybe even make some money, too.

RetailMeNot is a free app that offers deals from your favorite stores, coupons, gift cards, and cashback offers for both online and in-store shopping. You can save on clothing, jewelry, beauty products, electronics, and dozens more product categories. To make money while spending it, check out Ebates. Shopping with the Ebates app gives access to twenty-five hundred retail stores. These retailers give the website a commission on each item sold. Ebates then rebates some of that commission to its customers. Most large retailers such as Walmart, Macy's, and Best Buy also have their own mobile apps.

If you're looking for the best price on a particular product sold in numerous stores, there are price comparison apps that do the work for you. For example, ShopSavvy allows you to scan QR and bar codes and then find the best prices online and at local stores.

ally, you should check out products at various stores to find the lowest price. But driving around to several stores may cost more in inconvenience and gas money than you save on a cheaper product. Comparison shopping is made easy by websites such as NexTag, Shopzilla, and BizRate. Checking prices on retailers' websites may also turn up a bargain without leaving home.

Everyone loves getting a bargain, and teenagers are no exception. One way to find bargains is to shop at local secondhand stores, thrift shops, or garage sales. Gently used clothing at bargain prices can often be found there and can give you the satisfaction of sniffing out a deal on a unique pair of jeans or a cool shirt. Coupons can be found in newspapers, magazines, flyers

How Teenagers Shop

Generation Z—those born roughly between the mid-1990s and early 2000s—is fast becoming the target of marketers wanting to tap into the next big consumer generation. And it's no wonder: By 2017 Generation Z was contributing an astounding $44 billion to the US economy. Consumer reporter Eliza Brooke interviewed Generation Z high school students about their spending habits.

Nearly every student I interviewed is into buying clothes at thrift stores, whether that's because thrifting is cheap, because it helps you stand out from the crowd, or because it's better for the environment. Some . . . expressed deep wariness about capitalism and fast fashion, and enthusiasm for brands that prioritize diversity in their advertising. Pretty much everyone likes "retro" '90s styles like mom jeans and scrunchies.

The way that teenagers shop now is totally different than before—brands and trends mostly gain steam over social media—and yet still very much the same. . . . They're into clothes, makeup, and getting pizza with their friends. Gen Z considers the brands they support to be a reflection of their values, and the products they buy a way of telling the world how they wish to be perceived.

Eliza Brooke, "Juuls, Glossier, and Thrift Store Clothes: 6 High Schoolers on What They're Buying Right Now," Vox, September 24, 2018. www.vox.com.

that are mailed or hand delivered, and online. Seventeen-year-old Cole has used coupons to help out with his family's finances. "If I have a coupon for something I buy it," he says. "At first my friends teased me, now everyone wants to learn how."[16] Cole's shopping strategy includes scouring the internet for coupons. "You can actually get coupons online sent to you from all over the country," he says. "There may be better deals in Florida or New

York this week with higher value coupons so you get them from there but they apply to sales here."[17]

Perhaps the most widely promoted bargains come every year on Black Friday, the day after Thanksgiving. Prices are deeply slashed, and consumers rush to claim bargains. Online retailers have a similar day called Cyber Monday, when bargains are posted on the Monday after Thanksgiving.

Avoiding Spending Pitfalls

Most teenagers find that shopping is fun. After all, getting a brand-new outfit or the latest music download is a satisfying experience. But despite all the positive aspects of buying, there are some downsides to the shopping experience as well. If these pitfalls are not recognized and avoided, they can negatively impact even the best money management plans.

One of these pitfalls is our fondness for instant gratification, the desire to get something immediately. In an experiment conducted in the 1960s, four- and five-year-old children were given a marshmallow and told that if they did not eat it right away, they would be rewarded with a second one. Most immediately gobbled up the treat, while only a few were able to wait for the second marshmallow. This experiment pointed out the difficulty of waiting for something the child wanted, even though the delay would be rewarded.

Delaying gratification is important for more than just marshmallows: It is a key money management principle. "It's amazing to me how some people command incredible control over their desires," says entrepreneur Jen Monks. "People who successfully delay gratification believe they'll be rewarded for sacrifice. In addition, they're able to put more emphasis on future pleasures than immediate ones."[18] Although teens may be able to resist a marshmallow, they might have more trouble resisting a new outfit in a store window. But if purchasing that outfit puts a strain on your finances, it's better to wait.

> "There is more pressure to really belong and to dress a certain way. And certain groups only want you to wear certain clothes. If they don't like the way you're dressed, they'll make a comment like, 'Oh, that's gross.'"[19]
>
> —High school student Heather

Another financial pitfall comes from a source you may not realize you are influenced by: other teenagers. Peer pressure, whether subtle or obvious, can influence you in many areas, from smoking and drinking to craving the latest fashions. "There is more pressure to really belong and to dress a certain way," says Heather, a high school student in Anaheim, California. "And certain groups only want you to wear certain clothes. If they don't like the way you're dressed, they'll make a comment like, 'Oh, that's gross.'"[19]

One way to resist peer pressure is to go shopping alone. Shopping in groups places you under the direct influence of your peers, and you may be more likely to buy something you cannot afford just to fit in with the group. Having a budget—and the resolve to stick to it—is another way to combat peer pressure. Knowing what you can afford to spend and still remain on a budget is difficult but will go a long way toward healthy spending. Telling friends that "I just can't afford it right now" may be hard or even embarrassing. "I don't give in to peer pressure because I can't afford to," Heather notes. "I just wear whatever I'm comfortable in."[20]

Shopping Online

It probably comes as no surprise that the most popular shopping website for teenagers is Amazon. According to a 2018 survey by online market research firm Statista, 44 percent of teens questioned named the popular commercial website as their go-to place for internet shopping. One of the biggest advantages of shopping on Amazon, or any other commercial website, is the ease of buying almost anything online. But this advantage can also become one of its biggest drawbacks: It is too easy to make a purchase without thinking it through.

Teenagers are sometimes called digital natives: people who have always had the internet in their lives. While this makes them naturally comfortable with interacting online, it may also cause costly online mistakes. One of the most common mistakes is using a public Wi-Fi connection for online shopping. While convenient, these connections may not be secure, making personal information such as passwords and credit card or checking account numbers vulnerable to hacking.

Amazon is the most popular shopping website for teenagers. In a 2018 survey, 44 percent of teens named it as their go-to place for internet shopping.

Making sure that a retail site is reputable is another way to safeguard online purchases. Websites of well-known brands or stores usually list customer service phone numbers or email addresses so that problems with an order can be resolved. Be wary of amateur-looking websites, which could be a sign that the retailer is of questionable integrity or even a scammer. The seller may be difficult to contact, may send an item that is different from what was ordered, and may refuse returns or charge hefty restocking fees.

Most online retailers charge shipping and handling fees that, for small purchases, could be more than the price of the item ordered. There are usually several levels of shipping, with faster delivery costing more—sometimes a lot more—than standard shipping rates. Planning ahead and ordering early will eliminate having to choose an expensive rush delivery. Also, combining items into one order might put the purchase over the amount needed for free shipping.

Your email inbox is another potentially dangerous place. An email scam called "phishing" attempts to get unsuspecting recipients to click on a link that will take them to a page requesting personal information. While these emails may look legitimate, even using a recognized company's logo, they are often full of misspelled words and poor grammar. Closely examining a suspicious email could expose it as a fraud.

As with any activity, being knowledgeable makes for a better shopping experience. By learning the basics of smart shopping, teenagers will become adults who know that wise spending is a big part of sound money management.

CHAPTER FOUR

Credit: Use It Wisely

Money, in the form of metal coins or paper currency, has been used since around 700 BCE. But in 1950 a revolution began when businessman Frank McNamara handed a small card to a waiter after a meal. McNamara had agreements with several restaurants to accept delayed payment upon presentation of the card. He had formed a "diners club" of his friends, who each had their own card. The idea soon caught on, and by the end of 1951, forty-six thousand people were using Diners Club cards.

The Diners Club card is considered to be the first credit card. Others quickly followed, and by 2018 there were more than 416 million credit cards in circulation in the United States. "Credit cards are a vital part of the consumer credit economy,"[21] notes Matt Komos of the consumer credit organization TransUnion. Since teenagers are a big part of that economy, it is important that they understand the advantages—and disadvantages—of using credit.

Credit Cards

Credit cards are issued by banks and credit card services such as Discover, Mastercard, and Visa. Using a credit card is convenient, as blogger Eva Baker relates on the website TeensGotCents.

> "When I turned 18 earlier this year my dad helped me get my first credit card.... Even though I am only 18 I have already learned that just sliding a card is so much easier than pulling cash out of my wallet."[22]
>
> —Teen blogger Eva Baker

"When I turned 18 earlier this year my dad helped me get my first credit card. . . . Even though I am only 18 I have already learned that just sliding a card is so much easier than pulling cash out of my wallet."[22]

But having a credit card is more than just an easy way to spend money: It is a contract between the cardholder and the company issuing the card. When you use a credit card, you are actually getting a loan from the credit card company, and you agree to repay the loan at a future date. Ideally, you'll pay the balance on the card in full when you get the bill. If you make only a partial payment, what is left rolls over to the next month, and an interest charge is added. Unlike the interest that gives you money in a bank account or CD, interest charges added to a credit card account increase the remaining balance. Interest can be quite steep: In 2017 the average interest for cardholders with good credit was just over 17 percent. It is even higher for people with a history of poor credit management.

Teens who want to establish good credit often begin by being added as an authorized user to a parent's credit card account. As an authorized user, the teen can make purchases on the card, but the parent is fully responsible for the bill. This way the adults can keep track of their teen's spending habits and give advice when needed. Some cards have a minimum age limit for authorized users, often between thirteen and sixteen years old.

Secured Credit Cards

The next step may be a secured credit card, in which an amount of money, perhaps $500 or $1,000, is deposited in the card's account. This amount serves as security to limit the card issuer's liability. If the cardholder does not pay a bill, the money is taken from the account. A secured card is a good way to learn how credit cards work and budget money so as not to run out when a necessary purchase comes up.

Credit cards are issued by banks and credit card services such as Mastercard and Visa. When someone uses a credit card they are getting a loan from the credit company and are required to pay it off at a later date.

If you are eighteen years old or over and have a part-time job, you may qualify for a regular credit card in your own name. Such a card may have a low initial credit limit, perhaps $300 or so, but if you pay the monthly bill promptly, that limit will eventually be increased. As limits increase, however, so does the danger of credit running out of control. Leslie Baker, who has taught high school financial literacy classes, says some of her students "have already maxed out a $5,000 credit card and don't see a problem with that. They don't fathom how things like carrying a balance and finance charges really impact things."[23]

Debit Cards

Credit cards are not the only way you can make purchases on credit. Debit cards look like credit cards, often bearing a familiar Visa or Mastercard logo, and they offer the same convenience when shopping. But debit cards differ in that they are tied to a checking account; with each use, the amount of the purchase is withdrawn, or debited, from the account. When using a debit

My First Credit Card

Mikey Rox is a personal finance expert and blogger who knows from firsthand experience about the advantages and disadvantages of having credit cards. As soon as Rox turned eighteen, he received credit card offers from Mastercard and Discover. Thrilled at being recognized as an adult, he jumped at the chance and soon had two shiny new credit cards in his wallet. And that's when the problems began.

By his own admission, Rox didn't understand or care about the fine print that comes with a credit card. Soon interest at 23.99 percent and late fees began adding up. "Who cared about the fine print?" says Rox. "I didn't—and I paid for it dearly." Within months, his shopping sprees had taken his cards to their limits.

Rox was finally able to make deals with his creditors to pay his debts off at 50 percent of the balances. "I took the deals and was relieved to end the nightmare that I stupidly created, but the aftereffects lingered for several years more." His debt affected his ability to get loans, apartments, and even jobs. Rox's experience with his first credit cards motivated him to become a financial expert and to warn teenagers of the pitfalls of reckless charging.

Mikey Rox, "What I Did with My First Credit Card Is the Perfect Example of Why Teenagers Shouldn't Have Them," Business Insider, April 3, 2015. www.businessinsider.com.

---

card, you are using your own money, rather than the bank's money as in a credit card transaction.

Using a debit card avoids the danger of piling up interest charges. If there isn't enough money in your account to cover a purchase, the card will be declined. And debit cards provide a good way to keep track of funds: You write down card purchases in the checkbook log in the same way paper checks are recorded. One disadvantage of using a debit card is that, unlike a credit card, it does not help build up a good credit rating. Having a good credit rating makes a big difference in how much interest is charged when buying a car, house, or other major purchase.

Credit Ratings and Credit Scores

Everyone who uses credit accumulates a credit history, which details the number of credit cards you have, how much money you owe, whether bills are paid on time, and other factors. This information is collected by three financial reporting organizations: Equifax, Experian, and TransUnion. These companies create a credit report, which is available to banks, credit card issuers, utility companies, prospective employers, and others with a legitimate need to access your financial history. Banks, for example, use this information when considering loan applications. Once a year you can receive free copies of the reports to review them for errors that may affect your credit history.

Along with a credit report, there is also a credit score, calculated by a company called Fair Isaac Corporation (FICO). The FICO score is a number from 300 to 850 that indicates creditworthiness. "Your credit score is important," says financial expert Andrew Housser, "and a good score can significantly impact an individual's ability to borrow money. . . . Credit scores also can affect the ability to rent an apartment, lease a car, or even get a job."[24]

Good financial management, such as paying bills on time, results in a higher FICO score. People with lower scores pay a higher interest rate on credit cards and other loans or may be denied credit altogether. Only about one in five people will receive the highest scores of 800 or above and pay substantially less in interest.

Beware of Scams

Consumer credit is a billion-dollar industry, so it is not surprising that unscrupulous people invent scams to illegally obtain some of that hard-earned money. Teenagers who are new to using credit may be more susceptible to these swindles than adults who have years of experience in using credit cards. "Some scam artists know how to identify and take advantage of teens and their need

> "Some scam artists know how to identify and take advantage of teens and their need to fit in."[25]
>
> —Finance writer Janet Fowler

to fit in,"[25] says finance writer Janet Fowler on the Investopedia website.

Online scams top the list of dangers that teens need to be aware of. Even the most innocent-appearing messages can hide a ruse designed to take your money. One scam involved a Facebook post claiming that singer Justin Bieber was giving away free concert tickets, encouraging teens to click on a link. By doing so, however, they were taken to a site that signed them up for a premium service that cost eight dollars a week. Another online scam involved a phony movie casting agency claiming to get teens roles in a popular movie franchise. The catch was the requirement of an up-front payment for a casting session that never occurred or a high-pressure pitch to sign up for expensive acting classes with no guarantee of later employment.

Money scams can also occur at brick-and-mortar stores. For example, a diner may give his or her credit card to a restaurant

Online scams top the list of dangers that teens need to be aware of. Many of these scams involve getting someone to enter their credit card information before they realize they are being scammed.

The Future of Credit Cards

When is a credit card not a card? When you can wear it or use your phone to pay for purchases. These new technologies may herald a future in which physical credit cards are relics of the past.

Wearable payment devices include smart watches, fitness trackers such as Fitbit, bracelets, or apps on your smartphone that let you charge your purchases without using a credit card. Fitbit Pay, for example, uses your credit or debit card information when you make a purchase. Your card's reward points and bonus miles accumulate just as if the card was used, and transactions are encrypted for security. Apple and Samsung smart watches also allow for easy transactions without carrying credit cards, bills, or coins. A smart ring by the Token company can act as your credit card, as well as open your car and house doors.

You can carry an e-wallet rather than the typical leather one that is often bulging with junk and is vulnerable to theft. Also called a digital wallet, it is an app on your smartphone that allows payment at merchants with just a swipe of your phone near a store's wireless terminal.

server, who takes it back to the register and returns with the card and bill. While the card is out of the customer's possession, a dishonest employee could write down the card number and use it to make purchases before the scam is discovered. Even though most credit card issuers limit the liability caused by use of stolen cards or copied numbers, the danger of identity theft is always a concern.

Identity Theft

Our identity is linked to numbers found on Social Security cards, credit and debit cards, bank accounts, and other personal documents. These numbers, along with home addresses and computer passwords, should be treated as if they were money, because they are the gateways to your financial life. Identity thieves can steal this information and pretend to be you, draining your bank accounts, opening new accounts and running up enormous bills, and ruining a good credit history.

According to a 2018 survey, 16.7 million people were victims of identity theft in 2017, losing a total of nearly $17 billion. And adults are not the only victims of identity theft. "ID thieves love kids," says journalist and internet safety advocate Larry Magid, "because most have a clean credit record. And often teens won't find out that their identity has been stolen until they apply for their first credit card or a college loan."[26] Sometimes, identity theft is committed by someone known to the victim, perhaps a friend or even a family member. Personal identification numbers (PINs) and account information should not be shared, even with a relative or close friend, and should never be divulged to a stranger. Identity theft is most often perpetrated by strangers looking for someone who is careless about protecting financial information. It's important to shield your PIN when using an ATM, especially when strangers may be looking over your shoulder. Keep your Social Security card in a safe place at home or in a bank safe deposit box. When checking bank account information online, never use a public computer at school or a library because they are not guaranteed to be secure. Likewise, using a laptop, smartphone, or tablet at places like Starbucks or McDonald's is risky; unsecured Wi-Fi signals may be intercepted by identity thieves.

Finally, don't discard bank statements and credit card bills in the trash. Identity thieves often rummage through trash bins seeking account numbers and other information. Always shred financial documents before throwing them away. Use an inexpensive home shredder or take advantage of professional companies that provide shredding services.

CHAPTER FIVE

Debt: Learn the Pitfalls

Most adults understand that going into debt can be a necessary part of life. Few people have enough money to purchase a new house with cash or to finance a child's college education without relying on loans. But when debt gets out of hand, it can ruin a family's financial future. And it is not just adults who can get into financial trouble. Debt among teens is increasing, and eight out of ten college seniors will have at least some credit card debt by the time they graduate. Since teenagers are just learning the importance of financial planning, they usually do not have the experience to know how to handle credit or what to do if debt threatens to become overwhelming.

Getting Into Debt

When eighteen-year-old Ashlea got her first credit card, she racked up charges that quickly reached the card's credit limit. But that did not stop her. "It was like, 'This is maxed out, so I'll apply for another one,'"[27] she says. By the time Ashlea was twenty-three, she had accumulated ten credit cards and was $10,000 in debt. She ended up finishing college on a part-time basis so she could get a full-time job to pay off her debt.

> "Credit card companies have been pursuing teenagers and designing credit cards so they can 'learn' about the credit system. Credit card companies believe they have hit the jackpot."[28]
>
> —Credit expert Gary Herman

Ashlea's story isn't unusual. The ease of using credit cards and the scarcity of financial education in high school and college leave teens with little practical guidance for avoiding debt. One factor in the rise of teen debt is the proliferation of credit solicitations targeted at teenagers. "Credit card companies have been pursuing teenagers and designing credit cards so they can 'learn' about the credit system," says credit expert Gary Herman. "Credit card companies believe they have hit the jackpot."[28] Mailings or other offers touting easy credit often lead to a teenager obtaining several cards and piling up bills without realizing it. According to the *New York Times*, many banks partner with colleges and universities to offer students credit cards. Some of these cards even serve as student IDs. Many credit card issuers have used gimmicks such as offering a free T-shirt or other items to teens who sign up for a card.

Another way that teenagers get into debt trouble is misunderstanding the minimum payment that cards require for unpaid balances. Many teens do not realize how quickly hefty interest charges accumulate by paying only the minimum amount every month. Not paying a balance in full ensures that it will take years to pay it off.

Borrowing Money

Using credit cards isn't the only way to buy things on credit. For large purchases, loans from banks, credit unions, and other financial institutions may become necessary. One of the first major purchases many teenagers make is their first car. Of course, paying cash for a car would be ideal, but for most people, obtaining financing is necessary. Auto dealerships offer financing, but it pays to shop around for the best deal. A preapproved loan from a bank or other lender is based on credit history and FICO score to determine the amount to lend for a car. "Getting preapproved for an auto loan helps you set a realistic budget for your car purchase since you know how much you can borrow and at what interest rate,"[29] note finance and auto writers Lacie Glover and Philip Reed. Having a preapproved amount to spend is like paying with cash and gives the buyer a better negotiating position at the dealership.

Many college-bound teens will need to apply for education loans for tuition, fees, books, and other college expenses. The cost of a college education has been on the rise for years: The average tuition and fees for the 2017–2018 school year came to $9,970 at public colleges and $34,740 at private institutions. Grants and scholarships can lower these costs, but the remaining expenses must be borne by the students or their families.

There are several types of higher education loans available to qualified borrowers. The US Department of Education provides some $150 billion in funding annually, including loans, for more than 13 million college students. To receive federal funds, you must complete a form called the Free Application for Federal Student Aid (FAFSA). The government uses the information supplied

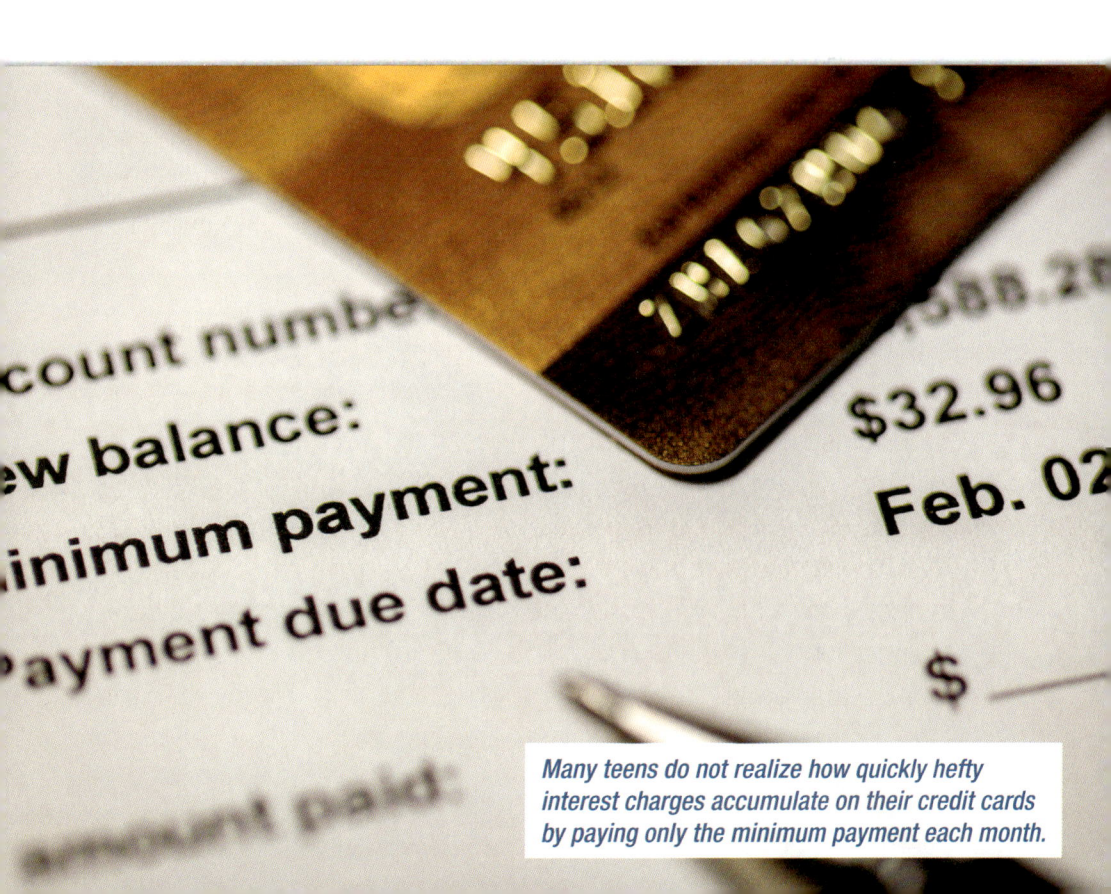

Many teens do not realize how quickly hefty interest charges accumulate on their credit cards by paying only the minimum payment each month.

in the FAFSA to determine the type and amount of monetary assistance you qualify for. This assistance may be in the form of grants or scholarships, which do not need to be repaid, or several types of loans, which must be paid back. Some two-thirds of college students rely on federal loans.

Federal education loans are categorized as either subsidized or unsubsidized. For example, the Stafford Loan is subsidized, which means that the government pays the interest during the time you're in school and for six months after graduation. After that, interest accrues and you must begin repaying the loan. Stafford Loans are available to undergraduate students who demonstrate a financial need. These loans have a low fixed interest rate, which for the 2018–2019 school year was just over 5 percent. Another subsidized loan is the PLUS Loan, which is offered to

Predatory Loans

Visiting a bank or other traditional financial institution is generally a safe way to get a loan for an unexpected expense, such as a hospital stay or major appliance breakdown. But sometimes people experiencing such situations become vulnerable to lenders that use dishonest or even illegal lending tactics in their loan offers.

Predatory lenders use deceptive or coercive practices to pressure a person into accepting loan terms that are unfair and often unaffordable to the debtor. These loans are usually issued for as few as thirty days, with astronomical interest rates of 100 percent or more. When a debtor can't repay the loan on time, interest and fees accumulate to drive the borrower even deeper into debt.

Payday loans, for example, are short-term loans that people use in a financial emergency. They are called payday loans because people plan on paying them back on their next payday. But at annual interest rates near 400 percent, many who can't pay are forced to get another loan to cover the first. It soon becomes a vicious cycle of debt that is difficult to escape. And it's expensive: Payday loan fees cost borrowers some $3.4 billion every year.

parents of college undergraduates or directly to graduate students. Interest rates are higher than for a Stafford Loan (7.6 percent in 2019), but the repayment plans are similar.

Unsubsidized federal loans are available to students regardless of their financial need. The school determines the amount of the loan, which is based on the cost of education at the institution, as well as other financial aid received by the student. Interest is not paid by the government, and repayment of an unsubsidized loan begins as soon as the loan money has been distributed.

Private loans, which are available from banks, credit unions, and other lending institutions, may be needed if federal loans do not cover all educational expenses. These loans usually have a higher interest rate, and the rate can change over time, in contrast to a federal loan's fixed rate. They may also be harder to get, since an applicant's credit history is taken into account. A poor credit history will mean a higher interest rate or the need for someone with a good credit rating to cosign for the loan.

> "I'm 26 and I graduated last year from Wright State with $25,000 in private loans and $20,000 in federal loans. . . . At this rate, I am petrified about never being able to afford a home or afford to have children."[30]
>
> —College graduate Joseph

Getting Out of Debt

For all the advantages of getting a college education, one of the biggest disadvantages is graduating with a mountain of debt. In 2018 some 70 percent of all college students graduated with some debt, averaging more than $32,000 per student—enough to buy a new car or put a down payment on a house. Such debt can upend a person's financial plans, create unhealthy levels of stress, and put hopes for the future in doubt. Joseph, a college graduate from Ohio, laments, "I'm 26 and I graduated last year from Wright State with $25,000 in private loans and $20,000 in federal loans. . . . At this rate, I am petrified about never being able to afford a home or afford to have children."[30]

Overspending, such as getting a loan for an expensive car, can lead to financial ruin. The way to avoid getting into debt is simple: Spend less money than what you earn.

Of course, college loans are just one kind of debt. Too much credit card spending, buying a car that is beyond your budget, or simply indulging in too much impulse buying can lead to financial ruin. The way to avoid getting into debt, for adults as well as teens, is simple enough: Spend less money than you earn. But getting out of debt already accumulated is more difficult. The first step in reducing debt is to examine your spending habits and cut down on unnecessary expenses. The money you spend on fast food, pricey lattes, and costly entertainment can be used to pay down debt. Bringing in extra income with a part-time job or making a craft that can be sold locally or online will generate additional income that can be put toward bills. Many teens have several credit cards, either from banks or from retail stores. Using only one card and canceling the rest can help keep debt from accumulating. Also, paying more than the credit card's minimum amount every month will make the outstanding balance disappear quicker and save on interest.

If a high interest rate is making it difficult to make a dent in credit card debt, it may be possible to negotiate a lower rate. A call to the card issuer can often result in a better rate, especially if previous payments have been made regularly and on time. In addition, money to help pay off debt can often be found by lowering auto insurance premiums with a higher deductible or by switching to a less expensive cell phone plan.

A Lesson in Debt

Chris is a college graduate who got into some serious debt. What he learned was a hard lesson about money and spending.

> I spent myself into a frenzy when I was in college. I spent so much money that I graduated with a car-sized student debt going to state schools. I did it in part to live like the kids I hung out with. I wanted to go home for the holidays. I didn't want to work full-time and go to school full-time. [In my family], education was important, recreation was desirable, and resources were available.

> I racked up a bunch of debt and then stopped paying for it. I couldn't possibly afford my private debt. The only reason I started paying back my student loans is because creditors finally got serious. My student loans are back on deferment [to postpone payments] as of now. My credit is ruined.

> We were taught to create debt. We have created debt and in doing so, we have taught our children to create debt. But debt usually has a creditor. But more important than the threat of a repo man is the empty fulfillment offered by the accumulation of debt and stuff.

Quoted in Tamsen Butler, *The Complete Guide to Personal Finance for Teenagers and College Students*. Ocala, FL: Atlantic, 2016, p. 177.

Handling Creditors

If a bill has gone long past due without payment, the creditor often contracts with a collection agency to resolve the situation. The methods used by collection agencies to collect debts run the gamut from a polite phone call to unscrupulous scare tactics such as verbal abuse, intimidation, and threats of arrest or confiscation of property. When Kathryn fell behind on payments for her Jeep Cherokee, a debt collector made repeated calls not only to her but to her father, sister, and other relatives. Calls to her brother at his place of work put his job in jeopardy. Kathryn even began receiving harassing posts on Facebook. She soon found out that she was not the only victim: The debt collector was threatening other people in the exact same way. She finally contacted a lawyer to represent her in a lawsuit against the collection agency.

Of course, by paying bills on time, you'll avoid having to deal with a debt collector. If bills do start getting out of hand, there are debt relief and credit counseling services that can help you create a plan for resolving outstanding debt. These organizations, both for-profit and nonprofit, offer advice on dealing with bills, consolidate loans, and help create a repayment plan that will eventually eliminate the debt. If the debt is so overwhelming that a person's income and other monetary sources have no chance of repaying it, these agencies may also provide advice on filing bankruptcy. A legal procedure, bankruptcy offers two ways to get out of debt. Under Chapter 7 bankruptcy, the debtor gives up some assets (such as bank accounts, a valuable coin collection, or a second car) to pay back creditors. In Chapter 13 bankruptcy, the debtor keeps the assets and sets up a three-to-five-year plan to repay creditors. Although bankruptcy should only be used as a last resort, it can give someone who is hopelessly in debt a chance to start fresh and, hopefully, practice better money management.

CHAPTER SIX

Investing: Increase Your Wealth

AAPL. NKE. PVH. XOM. These cryptic symbols are not part of some secret code but represent companies on America's stock exchanges. They are shorthand used by stockbrokers who buy and sell billions of shares of stock each day to investors seeking to make a profit. As you might guess, AAPL is the symbol for Apple, and NKE stands for Nike. PVH is a clothing corporation that owns fashion labels Tommy Hilfiger and Calvin Klein, and XOM is oil giant ExxonMobil. The three major US stock exchanges—NYSE, Nasdaq, and AMEX—list thousands of companies that offer stocks with share prices that in 2018 ranged from 15 cents for stock in software company Link Motion to a staggering $283,000 a share for financial conglomerate Berkshire Hathaway.

Although you may think that investing in stocks is only for adults, it can be a good way for teens to make some money while learning how the business world works. "The stock market has a boring and justifiably scary rep," says writer Melanie Mignucci in *Teen Vogue*, "but with caution and strategy, it's also a way to grow your money—and have some fun."[31]

How Stocks Work

When a company needs money to make new investments, expand research, or bring a new product to market, it may decide to raise that money by issuing shares of stock. Shares are actually tiny pieces of the company, and the people who buy them—the shareholders—become owners of a small part of that company.

> "The stock market has a boring and justifiably scary rep, but with caution and strategy, it's also a way to grow your money—and have some fun."[31]
>
> —Editor and writer Melanie Mignucci

Most investors use professional stockbrokers to advise them and to buy and sell stock, although shares can be bought online as well. Stock prices are listed on the US stock exchanges and are continually updated as their values change throughout the day due to economic, political, and other factors.

One way stockholders make money on an investment is through dividends. When a company is making a profit, some of that profit is given to its stockholders, usually on a quarterly or annual basis. If, for example, you own one hundred shares of stock valued at one dollar per share in a company, and that company declares a twenty-five-cent dividend, you would receive twenty-five dollars. You can spend it, save it, or reinvest it in the company by buying more shares of stock.

It is often stated that the goal for the successful investor is to buy stocks when their prices are low and sell them when prices go up. Sometimes, a company is so successful that its stock value skyrockets. For example, when cable TV giant Comcast first offered its stock to the public in 1972, one share cost $7. Someone who invested $1,000 in its stock back then would have had shares worth more than $1 million by 2018. Of course, not all companies are so successful, and prices can fall, reducing or wiping out a stockholder's investment.

Beginning to Invest

Even if you're not yet into your teen years, you can invest in the stock market. Parents can open a custodial account, which allows their child to buy and sell stocks under the supervision of the parents. Damon began investing in the stock market when he was just six years old, buying one share of Nike stock. That single $30 share became the basis of a portfolio worth $55,000 by the time he was nineteen. If you're eighteen years old (nineteen or twenty-one in a few states), you can legally buy and sell stocks. But before jumping into the stock market, you'll need to do some homework. "Smart investors research companies, mutual fund firms, and investment firms before they invest," advises the website Teens Guide to Money. "Not only do they need to understand the company and its future prospects, but also its industry, competitors, and how the company measures up to its competition."[32] Follow the ups and downs of the market on the internet to get a feel for how certain stocks that you might want to invest in are doing. Public libraries usually have numerous books written for teenagers about investing in stocks. Learn how the stock market works and the various ways of purchasing shares.

Media and cable company Comcast has had an impressive run since its initial stock offering as a public company in 1972. A $1,000 investment in the stock back then would be worth $1 million in 2018.

With the advent of the internet, online trading has become an easy way to enter the stock market. Online brokers such as E*Trade, Ally Invest, and TD Ameritrade handle buying and selling stocks for a small fee. Many offer free market research and other tools to help beginners navigate the often confusing world of stocks.

Risk Versus Return

Many teens start out buying shares of stock in their favorite companies, such as Coca-Cola, Apple, or Amazon. Companies like these are well established and not likely to go out of business,

An Investing Prodigy

Sudarshan Sridharan is a typical teenager except for one big responsibility: He manages some $250,000 of his parents' retirement portfolio. The Charlotte, North Carolina, sixteen-year-old has made some impressive money in the stock market, including shares of the electric automaker Tesla, which produced a $17,000 gain.

Sridharan became fascinated by stocks during his grammar school years. "My father told me to listen to *Marketplace* on NPR [National Public Radio]," he says. "And he brought investing books home for me. That's how I got interested." Sridharan made PowerPoint presentations to show his parents how he would invest real money, and soon they gave him a chance to invest in the market.

When Sridharan considers what stocks to buy, he has two criteria: "Will it be around in 10 years? Is this something that people need?" This strategy convinced Sridharan to buy Google, Microsoft, and Adobe stocks. "Those are three stocks," he says, "that if they went down, the Internet would just be in chaos."

For all his investing savvy, Sridharan has a healthy attitude about money. "I've realized that money isn't everything. It's just a tool to get you from Point A to Point B."

Quoted in Matt Egan, "16-Year-Old Made $43,000 on These Stocks in Three Years," CNN Business, July 26, 2016. www.money.cnn.com.

so their stock prices usually remain stable, making them low-risk investments. You're not likely to lose your money, but you won't make a bundle either. Other companies, such as cutting-edge technology firms, may bring higher monetary gains, but they do so at a greater risk of losing your money. Which stocks you choose to invest in should be determined in part by the risk involved.

Evaluating risk tolerance is an important part of investing. All investments include a certain amount of risk, and it's important to decide how much risk you are comfortable with. A person who is willing to lose money for a large but uncertain future gain is a high-risk investor. Someone who would be satisfied with a small monetary gain in order to keep his or her money relatively safe is a low-risk investor. In between are investments with various degrees of risk. The idea is often stated as risk versus return: Higher risks yield higher returns (that is, more money), while lower risks yield lower returns. There are several online quizzes available that will help you determine the level of risk you are willing to accept.

Low-risk investments include not only some stocks but bonds, which are issued by companies and municipalities to borrow money for projects such as new product development or highway improvements. Bond issuers pay back their borrowed funds with interest. Mutual funds are investments in which many investors pool their money to buy stocks from a group of companies, rather than choosing individual stocks. This spreads the investors' money among the companies, making the investment less risky. The safest of all investments is a bank account, which is insured by the government but pays minimal interest.

It is often difficult to tell whether a company will ultimately succeed or fail. For more than a century, Eastman Kodak was the dominant company for cameras and photographic film. But with the advent of digital photography and a camera in every smartphone, the company filed for bankruptcy in 2012. Similarly, the growth of Amazon led to the closing of many booksellers, and streaming services such as Netflix led to the demise of the Blockbuster video rental chain.

Diversification

Investors who buy only one stock can lose their investment if the company has a bad year or goes out of business. Successful investors rely on diversification to lower their risk in the stock market. Just like the old saying, "Don't put all your eggs in one basket," diversification means buying many different stocks, bonds, and other investments in order to spread the risk. "Diversifying your investments is important," says investment expert Mike Palazzolo, "because it's extremely difficult to know which investments will perform best. . . . When you diversify, you spread your investment across many companies around the globe."[33]

Diversified stocks can be a mixture of high-risk tech stocks, foreign stocks, established lower-risk stocks, and bonds. Regular savings accounts, CDs, and even precious metals such as gold coins will also help diversify a portfolio. The key is to choose investments in several areas. If your investment in a cutting-edge tech stock does well, you can make a lot of money. But if the stock tanks, you still have safer investments to cushion the loss.

In order to diversify, an investor must learn about the various types of investments available and which ones to choose to create a balanced portfolio. Fortunately, there are many sources of investment information, many of them free.

> "Diversifying your investments is important because it's extremely difficult to know which investments will perform best. . . . When you diversify, you spread your investment across many companies around the globe."[33]
>
> —Investment expert Mike Palazzolo

Getting Investing Advice

Not surprisingly, the internet is a good place to begin gathering advice about stocks. Many investment advisors use Twitter to dispense advice on buying and selling stocks. Financial expert Josh Brown delivers investment information to his more than 1 million Twitter followers. Jason Moser also gives investing ad-

One of the most interesting ways to learn about the stock market is through virtual trading. Many large brokers offer practice accounts that allow users to research, buy, and sell stocks without risking real money.

vice on Twitter, as well as on the radio and his own podcast. Other sites valuable to investors include the Motley Fool, Yahoo! Finance, and Investopedia, as well as online editions of *Forbes*, *Kiplinger's*, and the *Wall Street Journal*.

One of the coolest ways to learn about the stock market is virtual trading. Many large brokers offer practice accounts that allow users to buy and sell stocks without risking real money. "Most [practice accounts] are free," notes finance journalist Dayana Yochim. "The best give test drivers access to a fully functioning setup with the same tools that active customers use."[34] These stock market simulators are great for helping teenagers understand how the market works, but they are also used by experienced investors who want to try out new investment strategies without risking real money.

A Real Investment Club

Many high schools have investment clubs that employ simulation software games to teach teenagers the intricacies of investing in the stock market. In such games, profits and losses are on paper only, which can encourage unrealistic, reckless investing. But students at one private high school in Dallas, Texas, use actual money to play the market for real. And it is *very* real: Students have a pool of $100,000 to invest.

In 2013 the Business Club at Greenhill School was given the generous amount by members of the school's investment committee, made up of parents of current and former Greenhill students. Clint Golman, a Greenhill alumnus, says, "We thought that would provide a better learning experience than a game that was all about taking the biggest risk to win." With real money at stake, students are serious about managing risk and choosing stocks wisely.

Under club rules, students can invest only in companies worth $1 billion or more and must diversify their investments across six different industry sectors. No single company can represent more than 15 percent of the club's total investment. Any profits that the club makes will be used for Greenhill scholarships.

Quoted in Hibah Yousuf, "School Gives 16-Year-Olds $100,000 to Invest," CNN Business, June 13, 2013. www.money.cnn.com.

Investing for the Future

Investing with practice accounts can be fun, but playing the stock market for real is serious business. Warren Buffett, one of the world's most successful investors, purchased his first stock at age eleven in 1941. By 2018 he was worth some $84 billion, making him the third-richest man in America. Of course, not every investor will be as successful as Buffett. But beginning to invest early in life can bring rewards later.

Long-term objectives such as a college education, a house, or a comfortable retirement are worth investing money in. Not many teenagers think about retirement in high school or college, but it is an important investment goal. According to financial author Beth Kobliner, if a teen saves $1,000 a year in an IRA from age fifteen through eighteen, by age sixty-five that $4,000 investment will have grown to $107,000, even if he or she never saves another dollar. It takes time, but a little money can grow into a big payoff down the road.

Good financial management is an important skill that can make the present more enjoyable and the future more secure. And it's a skill that anyone can master with a little knowledge and a bit of discipline. The teenage years are a time of learning and discovery, when interests and talents are beginning to establish the adult that will soon emerge. They are a perfect time to become serious about personal finance and the important role it plays in the modern world.

SOURCE NOTES

Introduction: The Road to Financial Success
1. Neale S. Godfrey, *Money Still Doesn't Grow on Trees*. Emmaus, PA: Rodale, 2004, p. 7.
2. Quoted in Kathryn Tuggle, "Teaching Gap: 83% of Teens Don't Know How to Manage Money," Fox Business, July 17, 2012. www.foxbusiness.com.

Chapter One: Making Money: Build Your Income
3. Alison Doyle, "Job Search Tips for High School Students," Balance Careers, May 15, 2018. www.thebalancecareers.com.
4. Doyle, "Job Search Tips for High School Students."
5. Quoted in Susannah Snider, "The Pros and Cons of Having Your Teen Work a Part-Time Job," *U.S. News & World Report*, July 18, 2017. https://money.usnews.com.
6. Quoted in Snider, "The Pros and Cons of Having Your Teen Work a Part-Time Job."
7. Robert T. Kiyosaki, *Rich Dad Poor Dad for Teens: The Secrets About Money—That You Don't Learn in School*. Scottsdale, AZ: Plata, 2012, p. 43.
8. Quoted in Kara McGuire, *The Teen Money Manual: A Guide to Cash, Credit, Spending, Saving, Work, Wealth, and More*. North Mankato, MN: Capstone, 2015, p. 36.

Chapter Two: Budgeting: Plan Your Financial Life
9. Quoted in Aubrey Cohen, "Ways High Schoolers Can Start Managing Their Money," *USA Today*, April 29, 2015. www.usatoday.com.
10. Steve Scott, "Cash Envelope System: The Why and How for Implementing the Dave Ramsey Budgeting Template," Develop Good Habits. www.developgoodhabits.com.

11. Quoted in Tamsen Butler, *The Complete Guide to Personal Finance for Teenagers and College Students*. Ocala, FL: Atlantic, 2016, p. 80.
12. Thomas (TJ) Porter, "How to Open a Certificate of Deposit for Your Child," MyBankTracker, July 20, 2018. www.mybanktracker.com.
13. Pamela Capalad, "How to Make Budgeting Fun," *Teen Vogue*, June 15, 2017. www.teenvogue.com.

Chapter Three: Spending Money: Shop Sensibly
14. JCDecaux North America, "Teen Marketplace," 2016. www.jcdecauxna.com.
15. Erin Huffstetler, "Distinguishing Between Wants and Needs," Balance, June 13, 2018. www.thebalance.com.
16. Quoted in Radar Online, "Extreme Couponing Teen Says He's Addicted: 'It's like a Drug to Me,'" May 26, 2012. www.radaronline.com.
17. Quoted in Lisa Smith, "Local 18-Year-Old Featured on TLC's 'Extreme Couponing,'" WCPO, May 29, 2012. www.wcpo.com.
18. Jen Monks, "How Delaying Gratification Results in Remarkable Success," Life Wise Lady, December 15, 2016. www.lifewiselady.com.
19. Quoted in Karen Newell Young, "You Are What You Dress, Some Teen-Agers Discover at School," *Los Angeles Times*, May 5, 1989. www.latimes.com.
20. Quoted in Young, "You Are What You Dress, Some Teen-Agers Discover at School."

Chapter Four: Credit: Use It Wisely
21. Quoted in TransUnion, "Credit Card Usage at All-Time Highs, but Delinquency Rates Still Remain in Check," May 8, 2018. https://newsroom.transunion.com.
22. Eva Baker, "Should Teenagers Have a Credit Card?," TeensGotCents, 2019. www.teensgotcents.com.
23. Quoted in Jolene Gensheimer, "More Teens Dealing with Debt," ParentMap, June 1, 2005. www.parentmap.com.

24. Quoted in Butler, *The Complete Guide to Personal Finance for Teenagers and College Students*, p. 145.
25. Janet Fowler, "Common Scams Targeted at Teens," Investopedia, October 11, 2012. www.investopedia.com.
26. Larry Magid, "Teens Vulnerable to Identity Theft, Financial Crimes and Impersonation," *Forbes*, November 7, 2013. www.forbes.com.

Chapter Five: Debt: Learn the Pitfalls

27. Quoted in Catherine Valenti, "Rising Debt Among Young Worries Experts," ABC News, June 20, 2018. https://abcnews go.com.
28. Quoted in Consolidated Credit, "Teenagers and Credit Cards." www.consolidatedcredit.org.
29. Quoted in Lacie Glover and Philip Reed, "Why—and How—to Get Preapproved for a Car Loan," NerdWallet, July 2, 2018. www.nerdwallet.com.
30. Quoted in Max Filby, "In Their Words: Local College Grads Share Student Loan Horror Stories," *Dayton (OH) Daily News*, August 16, 2017. https://mydaytondailynews.com.

Chapter Six: Investing: Increase Your Wealth

31. Melanie Mignucci, "Tips for Teens on How to Invest," *Teen Vogue*, November 19, 2016. www.teenvogue.com.
32. Teens Guide to Money, "Teens Guide to Investing," 2019. www.teensguidetomoney.com.
33. Quoted in Jackie Lam, "Why It's So Important to Diversify Your Investments," *Zing!* (blog), Quicken Loans, November 9, 2017. www.quickenloans.com.
34. Dayana Yochim, "Virtual Trading: How Stock Market Simulators Work," NerdWallet, July 5, 2018. www.nerdwallet.com.

FOR MORE INFORMATION

Books

Tamsen Butler, *The Complete Guide to Personal Finance for Teenagers and College Students*. Ocala, FL: Atlantic, 2016.

Beverly Blair Herzog, *How Money Works: The Facts Visually Explained*. New York: DK, 2017.

Beth Kobliner, *Make Your Kid a Money Genius (Even If You're Not)*. New York: Simon & Schuster, 2017.

Omnigraphics, *College Financing Information for Teens*, 3rd ed. Detroit, MI: Omnigraphics, 2017.

Internet Sources

Aubrey Cohen, "Ways High Schoolers Can Start Managing Their Money," *USA Today*, April 29, 2015. www.usatoday.com.

eCampusTours, "How to Balance High School and a Part-Time Job," August 10, 2017. www.ecampustours.com.

Luke Landes, "The Best Investments for a Teenager," Consumerism Commentary, June 12, 2018. www.consumerismcommentary.com.

Melanie Mignucci, "Tips for Teens on How to Invest," *Teen Vogue*, November 19, 2016. www.teenvogue.com.

Chris Muller, "Budgeting for Teens—Grow Your Money While You're Young," Money Under 30, April 29, 2018. www.moneyunder30.com.

Websites

Investopedia (www.investopedia.com). This is a comprehensive website that covers all aspects of investing. It includes "Investing 101: A Tutorial for Beginner Investors" that will help new investors, including teenagers, navigate the complicated stock market.

MyMoney (wwwmymoney.gov). This website provides a variety of resources for teens, with links to games, financial resources, tax information, and money-saving tips.

Teens Guide to Money (www.teensguidetomoney.com). This website is a great source for financial tips and information aimed specifically at teenagers, from building a résumé to getting tips on smart shopping and advice for wise investing.

TheMint (www.themint.org). One of the best sites for all ages, TheMint provides financial management information for kids, teens, parents, and teachers. Sections for teens include tips for earning, saving, spending, investing, and safeguarding their money.

Games and Apps

Financial Football (http://practicalmoneyskills.com/play/financial_football). Visa has teamed up with the National Football League to produce this fast-paced, interactive game that teaches financial skills. The latest version features 3-D graphics and advanced football plays.

Honey (www.addhoney.com). With this free app, when you shop online Honey searches for and applies the best discount code for your purchases.

Moneytopia (www.saveandinvest.org/moneytopia). In this game, you keep track of finances with the ultimate goal of successfully managing your money throughout life, until you achieve your Big Dream.

Savings Calculator (https://tools.finra.org/savings_calculator). Use this handy financial calculator to determine the amount to save to reach your savings goal.

INDEX

Note: Boldface page numbers indicate illustrations.

Ally (online bank), 22
Ally Invest (online broker), 52
Amazon, 12, 30, **31**
Atack, Corbin, 16

Baker, Eva, 33–34
Baker, Leslie, 35
Balance (website), 25
bank accounts, 19–21
   online, 21–23
bankruptcy, 48
Bieber, Justin, 38
Black Friday, 29
Bliss, Jeff, 8, 10
bonds, 53, 54
Brown, Josh, 54
budgets/budgeting, 16–17, 22
   tools for, 17–18
Buffett, Warren, 56
Bushinski, Mik, 14
businesses, starting, 13

Capalad, Pamela, 23
car loans, 42–43
certificates of deposit (CDs), 21
comparison shopping, 26–27
coupons, 27–29
credit cards, 33–34, **35**
   secured, 34–35
creditors, 48
credit scores, 37
Cyber Monday, 29

debit cards, 35–36
debt, 41–42
Develop Good Habits (website), 17–18
Diners Club card, 33
dividends, 50
Dobroski, Scott, 10
Doyle, Alison, 8, 9

earnings
   deductions from, 13
   student, financial aid and, 10
Ebates (shopping app), 27
education loans, 43–45
envelope budgeting system, 17–18
E*Trade (online broker), 52
Etsy (website), 14
e-wallet (digital wallet), 39

Fair Isaac Corporation (FICO), 37
Federal Insurance Contributions Act (FICA), 13
FICO score, 37
financial aid, 45
   student earnings and, 10
Financial Football (interactive game), 62
financial goals, 6
   setting, 18–19
financial reporting organizations, 37
Fowler, Janet, 37–38
Free Application for Federal Student Aid (FAFSA), 43–44

Glover, Lacie, 42–43
Godfrey, Neale S., 4
Golman, Clint, 56
gratification, delaying, 29

Herman, Gary, 42
Hoberman, Judy, 5
Honey (online app), 62
Housser, Andrew, 37
Huffstetler, Erin, 25

identity theft, 39–40
interest
   credit card, 34, 47
   from savings accounts, 20–21
investment clubs, 56
Investopedia (website), 55, 61

JCDecaux, 24

jobs
    finding, 8–9
    part-time, pros/cons of, 10–11
    summer, 9

Kiyosaki, Robert T., 13
Kobliner, Beth, 57
Komos, Matt, 33

Magid, Larry, 40
McNamara, Frank, 33
Microsoft Excel, 18
Mignucci, Melanie, 49
minimum wage, 11–12
Mint (online app), 18
money
    borrowing, 42–45
    importance of, 7
money market accounts, 21
Moneytopia (interactive game), 62
Monks, Jen, 29
Moser, Jason, 54–55
Motley Fool (website), 55
mutual funds, 53
Mvelopes (budgeting software), 18
MyMoney (website), 62

needs, wants *vs.*, 24–25
New York Times (newspaper), 42

online banks, 21–23, **23**
online brokers, 52
online resources, 61–62
    for investing, 55
    for summer/part-time jobs, 9
online trading, 52
opinion polls. *See* surveys

Palazzolo, Mike, 54
paychecks, deductions taken from, 13
payday loans, 44
peer pressure, 30
phishing, 32
PLUS Loans, 44–45
polls. *See* surveys
Porter, Thomas, 22
predatory loans, 44

Quicken (budgeting software), 18

Reed, Philip, 42–43
RetailMeNot (shopping app), 27
Rusk, Isaiah, 14–15

saving/savings accounts, 19–21, 22, 54, 57
Savings Calculator (online app), 62
scams, 37–39
    online, 38
Scott, Steve, 17–18
shopping, 24
    with apps, 27
    avoiding pitfalls in, 29–30
    determining wants *vs.* needs and, 24–25
    online, 30–32
    smart, 26–27
spreadsheet programs, 18
Sridharan, Sudarshan, 52
Stafford Loans, 44, 45
Statistic Brain, 4
stock exchanges, 49
stock market investing, 49
    diversification and, 54
    getting advice on, 54–55
    getting started in, 50–52
    investment clubs and, 56
    risk *vs.* return and, 52–53
    virtual trading, 55, **55**
summer jobs, 9
surveys
    on annual spending by teenagers, 4
    on identity theft, 40
    on popularity of Amazon for online shopping, 30

TD Ameritrade (online broker), 52
Teenage Boss (TV program), 20
teenagers, annual spending by, 4, 5
Teens Guide to Money (website), 51, 62
TheMint (website), 62

wants, needs *vs.*, 24–25
Woo, Eddie, 20

Yahoo!Finance (website), 55
Yochim, Dayana, 55
You Need a Budget (YNAB, online app), 18